GOD'S
LOVE
FOR THE
REST OF US

VINCE ANTONUCCI

Tyndale House Publishers, Inc.
Carol Stream, Illinois

Visit Tyndale online at www.tyndale.com.

Visit Vince Antonucci at www.vinceantonucci.com and
www.godfortherestofus.com.

TYNDALE and Tyndale's quill logo are registered trademarks
of Tyndale House Publishers, Inc.

God's Love for the Rest of Us

Designed by Ron Kaufmann

Edited by Jane Vogel

Published in association with the literary agency of the Gates Group,
1403 Walnut Lane, Louisville, Kentucky, 40223.

Scripture quotations are taken from the *Holy Bible*, New Living
Translation, copyright © 1996, 2004, 2015 by Tyndale House
Foundation. Used by permission of Tyndale House Publishers, Inc.,
Carol Stream, Illinois 60188. All rights reserved.

Library of Congress Cataloging-in-Publication Data

Antonucci, Vince.
  God's love for the rest of us / Vince Antonucci.
    pages cm
  Includes bibliographical references.
  ISBN 978-1-4964-1058-0 (sc)
1. God (Christianity)—Love. 2. Christian life. I. Title.
  BT140.A585 2015
  231'.6—dc23   2015014939

Printed in the United States of America

21	20	19	18	17	16	15
7	6	5	4	3	2	1

CONTENTS

CHAPTER 1   Dead People   5

CHAPTER 2   Switching Sheets   29

CHAPTER 3   Coming Home   61

Now What?   71

Notes   75

1

DEAD PEOPLE

THERE ARE DEAD PEOPLE who are not fully dead. They're kind of alive. They're like walking dead people. And they're everywhere. It seems like every day there are more people who walk around like they're fully alive, but really they're mostly dead.

I'm talking about *real* life. But this does *also* happen to be what's going on in a movie called *Warm Bodies*.

Warm Bodies is set in a zombie apocalypse.* The main character is a zombie named R. He used to be human and alive, but now he's a zombie and mostly dead, and all he can remember of his name is the letter *R*.

R finds himself wanting to eat humans, but not only for physical sustenance. When he eats people, he experiences their memories, and it makes him feel alive for a moment. Really what R wants is to feel alive.

One day R sees a group of humans, and he finds himself attracted to a girl named Julie.** Later, when Julie is distracted by something, R eats her boyfriend. (Which is . . . one way to do it. The girl you like has a guy already? Eat him.) R's attraction to Julie grows, and soon

---

*I know that zombie movies are dark and weird, and that might make you uncomfortable. (It might make *me* uncomfortable!) But our culture's obsession with zombies may hint at a recognition that there's something dead about us. And it may help people to realize that what we need is new life. Stick with me on this movie illustration and you'll see what I mean.

**Not the way I'm attracted to Krispy Kreme donuts. He doesn't want to eat her; he wants to date her. The attraction is "romantical," as Mike Wazowski from the kid's movie *Monsters, Inc.* might say. (First a zombie movie; now a monster movie. Up next: a rabid-gerbil movie?)

he rescues her from the other zombies. To keep her safe, he takes her back to the abandoned airplane he lives in at an airport that is filled with hordes of zombies. And there are more of the "undead" arriving there every day.

That's how the movie begins, but I want to be clear: a few paragraphs ago I was talking about real life. There are people who walk around like they're alive, but they're mostly dead. They are walking, living, dead people. And there are more all the time.

Turns out it's always been that way.

You Will Surely Die

The Bible says it started back in the Garden of Eden. Whether we take the story literally or figuratively, either way God is teaching us something foundational about the human condition. We're told that God created two people, Adam and Eve, and he gave them Paradise to live in. He gave them only one rule. (Isn't that interesting? When God had the world the way he wanted it, there was only one rule. God is not into rules.)

God told them not to eat the fruit of one particular tree, the tree of the knowledge of good and evil. If they did, they would die.

You've probably heard the story. Adam and Eve were tempted. They screwed up and did the *one* thing they weren't supposed to do.

God had said the penalty for that was death. If someone made a movie today out of the story of Adam and Eve, this would be the point where you might get excited, because you're about to see two people die. You'd start to wonder, *How does God kill people?* And, *I can't wait to see what kind of special effects they're going to use to show them dying! Maybe it will be like that scene in* Raiders of the Lost Ark *where the people kind of melt before our eyes.* You'd be like, *Dude, pass the popcorn; Adam and Eve are about to get toasted.*

But if this were a movie, we'd be disappointed. Because it doesn't look like *anything* happened to Adam and Eve. God reprimanded them for what they'd done, and that's bad. They had to leave the garden paradise they'd been given, and that's bad. But they didn't melt before our eyes. And the earth didn't swallow them up. Adam didn't say, "Ooh, this is the big one! I'm comin' to join you, Elizabeth!" (*Sanford and Son* reference for the over-forty crowd.*) The big death scene didn't happen in this Adam-and-Eve movie. On the surface, the consequences don't seem tragic.

But Adam and Eve *were* dead. When they ate that fruit, when they talked to God later, when they walked out of the Garden, they were dead. They continued to walk around like regular people, but . . . they *were* dead.

We Are Like the Dead
And it's not just Adam and Eve. It's everyone since. We're all walking dead. The Bible talks about this quite a lot, like in Isaiah 59:10: "We are like the dead."

---

*If you're under forty, you can just ignore me. (Or you can insert a *Saved by the Bell* reference. Your call.)

You may be wondering, *What do you mean there are walking dead people? And in what way were Adam and Eve dead? And what does the Bible mean about* us *being dead people?*

Honestly, I'm not sure if I understand all this completely. In fact, I bet I don't. But I think I at least get parts of it. And I think the reality is this: we're all dead in all kinds of ways.

Emotionally Dead

For instance, I think many of us are dead— or at least pretty dead—*emotionally*. Can you remember moments in your life when you died emotionally? I can.

I grew up in a pretty crazy home. My father was a professional poker player in Las Vegas, a gambling addict, and a con man.* He was often in trouble, and our family was constantly run-

---

*Today, after growing up completely *not* as a Christian or churchgoer, I'm a pastor of a church in . . . Las Vegas. Yep, the very place where my father ruined his life and hurt so many people. When you give your life to God, he will write an amazing story with it.

ning from the consequences. He was also kind of an abusive jerk.

One of my earliest memories is a night when I was maybe five years old. I was asleep but woke up when I heard yelling downstairs. I ran down and saw my father in my mother's face, yelling. I was afraid of what my father might do to my mother, so I tried to pull him away from her. I couldn't move him, but I think my attempt embarrassed him. So instead of doing anything to her, he kicked me into the corner of the room and went after her most prized possession. It was the piano that her mother, who had died when my mom was in college, had left to her. He ripped a piece off it, threw it at my mom, and stormed out of the house. I looked and saw my mother lying on the floor clutching the piece of the piano, crying. I crawled over and tried to console her.

That night I didn't die *physically*, just like Adam and Eve didn't die physically that day in the garden. But I did die *emotionally*. I was in deep emotional pain, and I thought to myself, *I don't ever want to feel this way again. I would rather not feel anything than have to feel this way. I'd rather be dead than have to experience this again.* And I made a vow to myself that I would no longer care. I wouldn't get close to friends; I wouldn't trust my parents. My ability to experience the emotions I was intended to experience was seriously handicapped that night. I became a walking, living, dead person.

How about you? Do you have moments when you died emotionally?

Relationally Dead

I also think many of us are dead—or at least pretty dead—*relationally*. Somewhere along the line, someone or something killed our ability to trust people and have healthy relationships. As you can imagine, some of my father's actions did this to me. And I think even just moving a lot put some limitations on my ability to develop strong relationships. There have been lots of other things too—friends who didn't turn out to be what they seemed, girlfriends who did something behind my back. All of it led me to die relationally.

How about you? Perhaps you had a spouse who took vows committing to you forever, but forever turned out to be a lot shorter than you ever would have imagined. Or you had this coworker you trusted, but he or she completely broke that trust by taking credit for your work or stealing an account that should have been yours. Or maybe it was a parent who wasn't there. Or a boyfriend who said, "I love you," but he was just trying to get something from you.

Whatever, whoever it was, you've learned not to put your trust in people. Your heart has grown hard and cold. And the result is that you're sitting here today, dead.

Spiritually Dead

I think many of us are dead emotionally and many of us are dead relationally, and I *know* that many of us are dead *spiritually*. The Bible says in Ephesians 2:1, "Once you were dead because of your disobedience and your many sins."

This makes sense when you think about death as separation. In physical death, the body is separated from the soul. In emotional death, we are separated from our feelings. And in relational death, we are separated from other people. When the Bible says we're dead spiritually, what it's actually saying is that because of our "disobedience" and "many sins" we are separated from God.

God created us to live in a loving relationship with him. Maybe you've wondered, *What's my purpose? What is life all about? Why am I here?* You are here to love God and to be loved by God. *That's* your primary purpose in life, and that's a purpose worth living for. *That's* why God made you. *That's* his plan. His goal is to live in a loving relationship with you. And how awesome is that? It turns out we have a God who loves us and wants our love!

But there's a problem. For a love relationship to be authentic, each side has to choose to love the other. God has chosen to love you. The problem is, every person who has ever lived has chosen *not* to love God. We've all chosen *not* to do life in a relationship with God but instead to do life on our own.

At first blush you may balk at the idea that you've chosen not to love God. But look at your life. The Bible says that when we choose to do life in relationship with God, our top priorities will be loving him and loving people. Have those consistently been your top priorities? They haven't been mine. The Bible says that when we love God, we will be devoted to obeying his commands. Does that describe how your life has gone? Not mine. The Bible says that God should be the one we worship and trust in and turn to. Is that how you've done life? I haven't. And I think the truth is that we've all chosen to *not* do life in a relationship with God, but instead to do life on our own.

And God honors our choice. He's too much of a gentleman not to. Because we choose to do life on our own, we separate ourselves from God.

Maybe you realize that. Maybe that's why you're reading this little book. You don't feel close to God. God might be a concept you embrace, but he's not someone whose embrace you've ever felt. You don't experience God. You don't feel his presence or receive his guidance. What you feel is . . . separated from him.

We are like the dead. We're walking dead people.

Not only are many of us dead emotionally, relationally, and spiritually, but we're all dying *physically*. The statistics on death are pretty impressive—one out of one person dies.

You and I are going to die. We don't like to hear that or think about it or talk about it. In fact, we do all kinds of things to avoid thinking and talking about it. And we try to act like we're not scared of it, but we are.

Ever since we were kids, we've been acting

like we're not scared of dying. I think it starts at about seventh grade. When you're little, you don't mind expressing fear. Then you hit seventh grade and you're too cool, so you have to do things to prove that you're not afraid.

Ever watch a horror movie with seventh graders? They're laughing, going, "That's stupid. Ahhhh, look—his face is falling off!" You know why? Because they're scared kids trying hard to ignore the fear.

I have a friend named Tim who points out that this is also around the time when you start buying "shock your parents" music, which often revolves around death.

Every generation has to have a shock-your-parents kind of musician. Back when I was young, it was KISS. Parents were like, "I don't like KISS. It means Kings in Satan's Service." And it would shock our parents that we liked them, so we'd be all, "Ha, ha. They're my favorite band. That proves that I'm not afraid. I have no fear." Or there was Alice Cooper, who bit the heads off

things.* Or Ozzy Ozborne . . . who *also* bit the
heads off of things. Later, if you were a seventh
grader and wanted to prove how tough you were,
you'd go out and buy a Marilyn Manson album.

It's like there's a committee who approaches
this artist: "Sir, um, you're a musician, and well,
the seventh graders need a shock-your-parents
type of musician so they can feel tough. Could
you do it?" The guy sighs and says, "Yeah, I
guess I'll do it. Give me a rabies shot and something to bite the head off of." The committee
celebrates: "Yeah, we've got our man!"

Kids do all kinds of things to try to act like
they're not afraid of death.

And we still do it as adults. That's why we
don't think or talk about death. We pretend
we're not afraid of dying, but we are. And the
reality is that we *are* going to die.

So, now do you see what I'm talking about?
There are dead people. But they're not fully

---

*Actually, he didn't really. But everybody said he did, which in rock and
roll is pretty much the same thing.

18

dead. They're kind of alive. They're *walking* dead people. And they're everywhere.

Maybe you don't like to think of *yourself* that way. I'm sure you don't. But is it possible that you're dead and just haven't realized it? You've never come to terms with it, but there is a very real sense in which you're dead emotionally, relationally, and spiritually, and someday you'll be dead physically.

Kind of like the movie. These zombies, including R, are dead, but they're *walking* dead. Which sounds like the typical zombie movie, but *Warm Bodies* has a twist.

A Dead Person Comes Alive

You remember that R takes Julie back to the airplane he lives in. Well, in the airplane, they bond, and R finds himself coming back to life. Julie's love is slowly giving him new life.

In fact, there's a scene where *other* zombies see Julie and R holding hands, and even just *seeing* this act of love changes the other zombies.

Seeing love starts to slowly give them new life. Later, Julie and R find themselves in a situation where they're being attacked, and to escape, they have to jump into a pool far below them. When they come out, Julie kisses R, and that's when it happens. R is made alive. Her *love* brings him back to life.

A dead person *can* come back to life. Real love—even just *seeing* it—can start to slowly give a person new life. And I'm *not* talking about the movie. I'm talking about real life.

See, what the Bible tells us is that becoming a Christian is not about God making a *bad* person *good*; it's about making a *dead* person *alive*.[1] God resurrected Jesus from death to life, and he wants to do the same for us.*

---

*By the way, I used to think the idea that Jesus literally rose from the dead was a nice little myth that Christians conveniently believed in. Then I looked at the evidence. Yes, *evidence*. I actually came to believe in Jesus by studying the evidence. Many people have, including Harvard Law professors, scientists, archeologists, and a Pulitzer Prize–winning investigative journalist. If you're not sure about the Resurrection or the rest of the story the Bible tells, I would encourage you to examine the evidence. There are some great books that can help you with that, like *More Than a Carpenter*, by Josh McDowell; *The Case for Christ*, by Lee Strobel; and *The Reason for God*, by Tim Keller.

I want to make sure that gets tattooed on your brain. So please read it again:

Becoming a Christian is not about God making a bad person good; it's about God making a dead person alive.

And the Bible says that the way God does that is through *love*. God loves you. He's always loved you. And if you let him love you, God's love will bring you from death to life.

If you wanted to describe me at twenty years old, *dead* would have been a great word. I was dead emotionally, relationally, and spiritually. But I found God (or God found me), and I let him love me, and he dramatically changed my life. He's resurrected me from the dead. He's made me alive and given me new life. I'm not completely where I need to be yet, but the more I let God love me, the closer I get.

When you let God love you, he goes to work in your life resurrecting you spiritually, emotionally, and relationally. And as you let God pour his love into you, his love will start to spill out of you, allowing others to experience God's love through you. In fact, Jesus said that people would come to know him through seeing the love his followers have for this world and especially for each other.[2] Even *seeing* real love can start to slowly give a person new life.

That's the idea of Christianity.

You may be thinking, *No—I know about Christianity and about Christians, and it's not about love. It's about boycotts, politics, and judging people.* I understand why you feel that way, because there are some Christians (or people who call themselves Christians) who do it wrong and give Christianity a bad name. And I apologize for that. But that's not what Christianity is about. Don't let some messed-up people keep you from experiencing the thing you really need, which is the love of God that will make you alive and give you a new life.

Let's look at what the Bible says in a book

called Ephesians. Ephesians 1:18 reads, "I pray that your hearts will be flooded with light so that you can understand the confident hope he has given to those he called—his holy people who are his rich and glorious inheritance."

The prayer here is that we would understand the value God places on us. Yes, we've screwed up. Yes, we're messed up. But in a sense, it doesn't matter. Because God still views us as treasures. We're "his rich and glorious inheritance."

That passage continues in Ephesians 1:19-20: "I also pray that you will understand the incredible greatness of God's power for us who believe him. This is the same mighty power that raised Christ from the dead and seated him in the place of honor at God's right hand in the heavenly realms."

The power God uses in our lives and makes available to us is incredibly great. It's "mighty power." It's the power God used to raise Jesus from physical death to new life on the first

Easter Sunday. He now uses that same power to raise us from spiritual death to new life.

Why? Why does God make this offer to us? In the next chapter we read, in Ephesians 2:4-5, "God is so rich in mercy, and he loved us so much, that even though we were dead because of our sins, he gave us life when he raised Christ from the dead. (It is only by God's grace that you have been saved!)"

The Bible says God did this because "he loved us so much." God's love is not just for the good, the pious, the religious. God's love is for the rest of us. God's love is for *you*.

It says that God is "rich in mercy." His posture toward you is not one of condemnation, but of compassion.

It says we are saved "by God's grace." Grace means getting something better than you deserve. We've screwed up, we're messed up, but it doesn't matter, because of grace.

The Bible says that by grace we have been "saved." I'm going to get real geeky for a minute. I apologize for this, but my mother was an English teacher. In Greek, the original language of the New Testament, that word "saved" is written in the perfect tense.

Do you remember from school that verbs can be past tense, present tense, future tense, or a perfect tense?

Past tense indicates something that has already happened.

Present tense indicates something that is happening right now.

Future tense indicates something that will happen eventually but hasn't yet.

The perfect tense in Greek refers to something that has happened in the past but has an ongoing impact in the present and into the future. Using the perfect tense draws attention to the continuing effects of something that has happened in the past.

And *saved* is written in the perfect tense. How cool is that?

The idea is that you were saved from death,

from being separated from God, all at once in the past, but the effect of that is continuing in your life. God will continually do his resurrecting work in your life until it's finally complete.

That means you never have to feel defeated, and you should never give up!

You may have "gotten saved" awhile back, and you're confused because there are still parts of your life where you feel dead. Don't lose hope. God is perfect, his love for you is perfect, and he saved you in the perfect tense. That means his work in you isn't done yet! God is still at work in you, bringing life out of death.

On the cross, Jesus died and absorbed our death. Then he defeated our death by his resurrection. And that same resurrection-from-the-dead-kind-of-power is available to you.

God can love you from death to life.

He wants to love you.

The only question is: Will you let him?

Will You Let Him?

A pastor named Michael Brown tells a story that illustrates God's love and the choice we have in how to respond to it:

> A friend told me about a boy who was the apple of his parents' eyes. Tragically, in his mid-teens, the boy's life went awry. He dropped out of school and began associating with the worst kind of crowds. One night he staggered into his house at 3:00 A.M., completely drunk. His mother slipped out of bed and left her room. The father followed, assuming that his wife was in the kitchen, perhaps crying. Instead he found her at her son's bedside, softly stroking his matted hair as he lay passed out drunk on the covers. "What are you doing?," the father asked, and the mother simply answered, "He won't let me love him when he's awake."[3]

The question is: Will you let God love you?

Will you accept the possibility that you're dead? And that what you need more than anything is for God to love you, to bring you back to life.

God wants to love you.

Will you let him?

2

SWITCHING SHEETS

SHE ASKED if I'd go talk to her mom, who was dying in the hospital. I was her pastor. Of course I said yes. I asked if her mother *wanted* a pastor to come. Did she go to church? Did she believe in God? "Not really." "No." "Not so much."

I showed up feeling a little apprehensive. Forcing myself on people isn't my favorite thing. But I had visited with people on their deathbeds before. I was prepared for that. What I wasn't prepared for was the mask jacketing her face to help her breathe. The fact that she looked like she could pass at any moment made the steady beep from the monitors sound like a funeral dirge.

As I was being introduced, I heard something. It was coming from behind the mask. She was saying something. Whatever it was, she was saying it over and over. I leaned in and was able to discern her words.

"I don't want to die. I don't want to die. I don't want to die."

Who does?

I don't think anyone wants to die. Well, actually, I take that back. I have met one brave soul who seemed to truly have no fear of death. He was short, hairy, and liked to lick his own butt. He was a dog I used to have, a beagle– springer spaniel mix named Buster. Buster had a death wish.

There was the time we left a gigantic tub

of chocolate-chip cookies on the counter and went out for a few hours. While we were gone, Buster somehow managed to get up on the counter. I have spent years analyzing how a dog whose top height was about eighteen inches off the ground could get up on a four-foot-high counter. I have come to no conclusions.* But he did it. And he ate *all* the chocolate chip cookies.

When we got home and saw what had happened, my wife, knowing that chocolate is poisonous to dogs, cried out, "Oh no! My puppy!" I, knowing that chocolate is delicious to eat, cried out, "Oh no! My cookies!"

We didn't know what to do about the fact that our dog had eaten all those chocolate-poison cookies, and I was pretty upset about losing the cookies, so we did nothing. And

---

*However, I suspect the answer involves a lot of gymnastic training at the Olympic facility in Colorado Springs. How Buster was able to fit gymnastic training into his already tight schedule of sleeping, barking at neighbors, and licking his butt, I have no idea. How he was able to afford this training is a whole other brain twister.

Buster seemed fine until he started throwing up . . . chocolate milkshakes. His body couldn't handle the chocolate, so it started ejecting it all over our apartment.

I had cleaned up Buster's vomit before, and it was always gross, but there was something different this time—it was pure chocolate, and it looked really tasty. And it smelled great. I realized I was drawn to it, and then I was totally grossed out!

Buster tried to give new meaning to death by chocolate. Then there was the time he jumped out of a second-story window. And the time he ran into the middle of a road and was hit by a car. I could go on. Buster had no fear of death.[1]

The rest of us are more like that woman in the hospital room. We don't want to die.

But there's a problem. Death is coming. As I said before, the statistics on death are very impressive: one out of one people die. And we need to be ready.

We want to overcome our "walking death" and experience real life in this life, and we need to be prepared for whatever happens after this life. People wonder what happens next. Is there really a Judgment Day? A heaven? A hell?

I'm always hesitant to talk about death and what comes after, because I don't want to seem like one of those crazy doomsday people or one of those too-intense, hellfire-and-brimstone guys who seem to have no compassion. But, well, death and whatever comes after it *are* coming. So we need to be ready. And maybe we could even get to a place where we're not afraid to die or of what comes next.

So let's pretend you've just died and it's Judgment Day. (Yikes!) I want to give you two questions you'll want to have figured out by then. In fact, I'd like you to think about how you'd answer these two questions right now. Then I'll share some important ideas from the Bible with you. Then I'll ask the two questions again. And we'll see if maybe your answers change.

So you've died and it's Judgment Day. You're standing before a holy, righteous, just God. Question #1: What is your chance of getting into heaven? The Bible says that there really is a perfect place called heaven and another not-so-perfect place called hell, and some people are going to heaven and some are going to hell. So what's your chance of getting into heaven on Judgment Day? You could say 0 percent, 1 percent, 2 percent, 5 percent, 50 percent, all the way up to 100 percent. What chance would you give yourself if it were Judgment Day right now? _____ percent

Question #2 is related to the first, but different. This question comes directly from God. You're standing there on Judgment Day, he looks you in the eye, and asks, "Why should I let you into my perfect heaven?" How do you answer that question? What would you say to God?

By the way, I don't know for sure, but I think it's very possible that God *is* going to ask that question (or a question just like that), so it's probably something you should think about and prepare for.

So, there are two questions. Do you have your answers?

I need to tell you that I believe that there are only two possible answers to the first question and only one correct answer to the second question. *Many* people give wrong answers to each of those questions. So let's think about some of the mistaken ideas that could lead us to give those wrong answers.

Mistaken Idea 1: The Standard by Which We'll Be Judged

In response to the question "What do you think are your chances of getting into heaven?" a lot of people say, "Fifty–fifty" or "Eighty–twenty." Why? Because they're comparing themselves to their neighbors or to some murderer they've seen on TV. We look around to others as our standard, and we say, "Well, my chances have to be pretty good, because I'm a pretty good person. I'm definitely in the top half. Probably in the top quarter."

But that's *not* the standard. God's standard is *perfection*. The Bible tells us that the standard God has for our lives, the standard we have to meet to be in a relationship with a perfect God, and the standard we have to meet to get into a perfect heaven, is perfection. Not pretty good, not good, not even really good. Perfect.

I don't know if you're into bowling or have spent much time watching bowling on TV*, but maybe you've seen someone go for a perfect game. Let's say this guy is going for a perfect game, a 300. He gets eleven strikes in a row, and then on his twelfth roll, a 9. Now to the uninitiated, that's a great game. But if your goal is a perfect 300 game, it doesn't matter if you get a 299 or a 199 or a 99 or a 9. It's not perfect.

Another way to think about this: say you're

---

*And if so, get a life!

hanging from a cliff by a chain. *Every* link of that chain has to be perfect for it to hold you up. Right? If one link breaks, it's no longer perfect. And you wouldn't say, "Well, almost all of the links are good." No—it doesn't matter if it's one link or many; it has to be perfect.

To measure up to God's standard for getting into heaven, we have to be perfect. Why?

Well, there are lots of reasons.

One is that if heaven is a perfect place (and it is), then to allow something imperfect into heaven would mar the perfection. Think of it this way: you have a perfect, flawless, brand-new car, and you allow a smelly, muddy dog in it. Your car is not going to be flawless anymore, is it? In the same way, if God allows something imperfect into heaven, everything will be tainted.

Another reason is that it isn't safe for an imperfect person to be in a perfect place with a perfect God. The Bible often compares God's holiness and perfection to a fire that is so white-hot that it burns up anything that is not perfect and holy.[2] Imperfect people simply can't survive in a perfect heaven with a perfect God.

And we're not perfect.

Mistaken Idea 2: Not Understanding Our Own Sinfulness

That's the second mistaken idea we might have that can lead us to give some wrong answers. We tend to underestimate our own sinfulness. (There's that *sin* word you were wondering about/waiting for.)

The Bible tells us that God has a perfect plan for each of our lives. That plan includes how we should live.[*] The problem is that each of us has chosen, through the free will that God has given us, to go against God, to rebel against his plan, to not live the way he's asked us to live.[**] That's what the Bible calls sin. One of the

---

[*] At its core, God's plan is for us to love him and to love people and put them before ourselves.

[**] At its core, our sin is selfishness. Rather than living for God and others, we live for ourselves and our own desires, success, and happiness.

words the Bible uses for *sin* actually started out as an archery term. It means to miss the mark, miss the bull's-eye, miss perfection. The Bible writers use it to describe missing the mark of God's perfect plan for our lives.

We've all done that. The Bible tells us in Romans 3:23, "Everyone has sinned; we all fall short of God's glorious standard." Every one of us has missed the mark. I'm not pointing fingers. I'm right there with you. We've all sinned.

And we've all sinned *far more often* than we could ever imagine.

The Bible talks about at least two broad categories of sin: sins of *commission*, which happen when you do something you know you're not supposed to do, and sins of *omission*, which happen when you know something you should do, but you do not do it.

We've all done things we knew were wrong, and we've all failed to do things we knew we should have done. We all fall short of the standard.

But it gets even worse. Because Jesus taught that if we even *think* something, in God's eyes it's the equivalent of doing it. Jesus basically said, "If you think, 'I'd love to kill that guy,' well then, you did, in your heart." He also said, "If you look lustfully at a woman, you've committed adultery with her in your heart." All those wrong thoughts count.[3] They're also sin.

We have sinned more than we could ever imagine.

And our sin is *far worse* than we can imagine. We just don't see it as that bad, because our standards are pretty low. It's like a person who knows almost nothing about music listening to a very average band. He's not going to notice the imperfections. He might think the band's pretty good. But if a musical virtuoso listens to an average band, she'll notice all the imperfections. She'll think the band is pretty bad. When we look at ourselves or our friends, our sins don't look so bad to us. But when a perfect God looks at us, our sins look *really* bad.

And it's not just that our sin is being evaluated by God; it's also that we're sinning *against God*. And that really matters. Author David Platt tells a story that illustrates what I mean:

Azeem, an Arab follower of Jesus and a friend of mine, was sharing the gospel recently with a taxi driver in his country. The driver believed that he would pay for his sin for a little while in hell, but then he would surely go to heaven after that. After all, he hadn't done too many bad things.

So Azeem said to him, "If I slapped you in the face, what would you do to me?"

The driver replied, "I would throw you out of my taxi."

Azeem continued, "If I went up to a random guy on the street and slapped him in the face, what would he do to me?"

The driver said, "He would probably call his friends and beat you up."

Azeem asked, "What if I went up to

41

a policeman and slapped him in the face? What would he do to me?"

The driver replied, "You would be beat up for sure, and then thrown into jail."

Finally, Azeem posed this question: "What if I went to the king of this country and slapped him in the face? What would happen to me then?"

The driver looked at Azeem and awkwardly laughed. He told Azeem, "You would die."

To this Azeem said, "So you see the severity of sin's punishment is always a reflection of the position of the person who is sinned against. The driver thus realized that he had been severely underestimating the seriousness of his sin against God."[4]

We all tend to do that. We don't understand our own sinfulness, partly because we don't understand God's holiness.

The other thing we don't understand about

our sinfulness is that sin is not just a legal issue. It's a *relational* issue. We think of sin as just breaking laws. It's not. Let's say you were speeding down the road, and a cop pulls you over. He gives you a ticket because you broke the law. But it doesn't hurt the cop's feelings. Right? He doesn't look at you with tears in his eyes and say, "How will we ever recover from this?" Why? Because it's just legal; it's not relational.

But if I sin against my wife—let's say I commit adultery—I haven't just broken our wedding vows; I've broken her *heart*. She *would* look at me with tears in her eyes and ask, "How will we ever recover from this?" Because that sin would be relational.

When we sin against God, it's not just legal. It's *relational*. We're not just breaking laws; we're breaking his heart.

People often say, "I'm a good person, so I'm sure God accepts me" or "I'm a good person, so I'll go to heaven when I die." Maybe you've said that. Well, people who say that don't understand that it's *not* just about good and bad. Sin isn't just legal; it's relational. Sin is a rejection of relationship.

Think of it this way: Imagine a woman—a poor widow—with an only son. She loves him. He is her world. As he's growing up, she teaches him how she wants him to live: to always tell the truth, to work hard, and to help the poor. She makes very little money, but with her meager savings she is able to put him through college. Imagine that when he graduates, he almost never speaks to her again. He occasionally sends a Christmas card, but he doesn't visit her; he won't answer her phone calls or letters; he doesn't speak to her. But he *does* live like she taught him—he's honest and works hard and is generous with his money.

Would you say that's acceptable? Of course not. We would say that though he is acting like a "good person," actually, by neglecting a relationship with the one who gave him life, the one to whom he owes everything, he is living a life that is condemnable.

God created us for relationship with him, and he loves us. We owe him everything. If we try to "live good lives," but we don't love him or live in relationship with him, it's simply not enough. God loves us and made us to be in relationship with himself, not just to be good people.

So if you think that God accepts you and you'll go to heaven because you're a good person—no. First of all, you're not that good. You've sinned far more often and your sin is far worse than you could imagine. (Just like me and mine.) And second, it's not about being a good person. It's about having a relationship with the God who continually reaches out to you in love. If you're a good person but reject the relationship, that's not commendable; it's condemnable.

Heaven is the place where people go to be with God. It's the place for people who want to live in a relationship with God. See, God gives each of us a choice: Live my way, be in relationship with me, and someday spend eternity with me; or go your own way, break off the relationship with me, and choose to spend eternity apart from me.

Throughout the Bible, God lets us know that it breaks his heart that we would choose against him, but he won't force us to choose him.

So . . . why do you have to be sinless? Because when we sin, we basically tell God, "I'm going my way. I don't want to follow you. I want to do my own thing. I don't want a relationship with you." And God allows it, even if it breaks his heart.

This is why it's wrong to say that God sends people to hell. God doesn't send people to hell. People *choose* hell. Hell is the fulfillment of a person's choice to go his or her own way and to be apart from God. God is the last person who wants anyone in hell, but he will not force us to be with him in heaven.

I wonder how many people have stayed away

from church because they felt like they could never be good enough. Would they be more interested if they knew it was about relationship, not religion?

I think of Sandy, a Britney Spears impersonator on the Vegas Strip. She went to church a few times growing up and a few more as an adult. She never went back to the same church twice. Why? She never felt like she could measure up. The people there seemed so holy and pristine. She knew she wasn't. She felt like they were looking down on her from their pedestals. She could never be good enough.

I guess, in a sense, she at least had that going for her. She knew she was a sinner and that her sin was bad.

The second misunderstanding many of us have that might lead us to incorrect answers for the two questions is that we don't understand our own sinfulness, how much we've sinned, how bad our sin is, that it's not just legal—it's relational.

Another reason goes back to the idea that sin is relational. I used to think, *If there is a heaven, I think I'll go there when I die, because even though I haven't really lived my life with God, I'm a pretty good person.* I totally didn't get it. Heaven is the place where people go to be with God. It's not the place for good people; it's the place for people who want to live in a relationship with God.

Mistaken Idea 3: God's Offer
This leads to the third misunderstanding we often have.

We don't understand God's *offer*. God is love. God loves you. And God's love leads him to make this offer to you by his grace.

I have this theory that when we come into existence, a piece of paper comes into existence along with us. This paper has a line drawn down the middle. Mine, for instance, has "Good things Vince has done" on one side and "Bad things Vince has done" on the other. Your sheet has your name. Throughout our lives we've been putting things on the good side. Like me, for instance:

- Once, when I was little, I drew my mom a nice picture. That goes on the good side.
- And I've been nice to lots of people. Put that on the good side.
- And I've helped out quite a few people in different ways. That goes over there.
- I'm usually pretty nice to my wife. You can ask her. Chalk another up for Vince.
- I had a dog I took pretty good care of. Put that down.
- I've started two churches. That must be good.

And I've got some other things on the good side. But you know what? Throughout my life, I've also been putting things on the bad side.

- There were a lot of times when I disobeyed my mom. I guess that goes on the bad side.
- I've been accused a few times of being a jerk to people. I can't deny it. That's on the bad side.
- I would be ashamed to tell you some of the things that I've done to people. I won't get specific, but those go on the bad side.
- There have been times when, in anger, I have intentionally made my wife feel bad about herself. Bad side.
- At least once or twice, in frustration, I kicked my dog. That has to go on the bad side.*
- I helped start two churches that have done well, but sometimes I take some of the glory for myself, when I know it's God who has done it all. That goes there.

*If I had kicked a cat, I'm not sure which side it would go on. (I kid! I kid!)

Each of us has a sheet like that. The more honest of us would admit that our list of bad things would require *reams* of paper. So someday you stand before God on Judgment Day. He asks, "Why should I let you into my perfect heaven?" You have your sheet. He takes it from you and starts looking it over. He says, "Well, these good things are good. I loved watching when you chose to love and do good. I'm proud of you. I'm glad you did those things. But, what about this side?"

You say, "Yeah, but did you notice I was in Girl Scouts? I sold a lot of Thin Mints! And what about that time I . . ."

And God says, "Yes, I know, but what about this side? You've got quite a list here of bad things. And you see, even if you just had one bad thing on your list, I couldn't possibly let you in, because my heaven is a perfect place. I'm sorry."

See, we each have a recording of our good things and bad things. And the bad-things side is the part that puts us in a really bad situation.

But check this out: Jesus came and lived on the earth for about thirty-three years. In his life he also had a sheet. One side said, "Good things Jesus has done." The other, "Bad things Jesus has done." In his life here on earth, Jesus just piled good things on the good things side: healed leper; showed grace to immoral tax collector; fed five thousand hungry people. Jesus had a tremendous good side.

But what's truly remarkable is that under "Bad things Jesus has done," there's nothing. Jesus was absolutely sinless. He was the one and only person to live an entire life on earth without missing the perfection mark. In fact, the people who spent the most time with Jesus and who would have most clearly seen his sin, if he ever did sin, asserted that he was sinless. His buddy John wrote in 1 John 3:5, "There is no sin in him." His close friend Peter wrote in 1 Peter 2:22, "He never sinned, nor ever deceived anyone."

Even Jesus' *enemies* agreed that he was without sin. At Jesus' trial, Pontius Pilate said, "This man has not sinned." At Jesus' crucifixion, the military official in charge stated, "This is a righteous man." We're told it repeatedly: Jesus never sinned. He had nothing under "Bad things Jesus has done." That's why God can make his grace offer, which so many of us misunderstand.

Let me try to explain it.

Picture an old movie with a mad scientist as a character. He has a man strapped into a bed. Strapped into another bed is a duck. Both have wires taped to their heads. Lightning strikes, the mad scientist pulls a lever, and some electric buzzing happens. Suddenly the man is going, "Quack, quack, quack," and the duck says, "The hypotenuse of a right angle . . ." You realize that somehow there was a switch.

Here's God's offer. God says, "Despite the fact that you have rebelled against me and fallen far short of my standard of perfection, I love you. You aren't perfect, but my love for you is. It's impossible for you to take away the bad things you've done or to add enough good things to your list to make up for all the bad things. But because of my love for you, I want to offer you a gift. The gift is this: I will switch the sheets. If you will accept my gift of grace, I will go back in time to the cross, to the moment when my Son was crucified, and I will switch your sheets."

So your sheet. Jesus' sheet. Switched.

God says, "Through his death on the cross, Jesus will take all your sin. And you will receive his perfect bad-things side. I will look at you, from now on, in this life, on Judgment Day, and through all eternity, as if you've never sinned. If you accept this grace gift I'm offering to you, I will switch your sheets."

We find one of the ways the Bible expresses this idea in 2 Corinthians 5:21: "God made Christ, who never sinned, to be the offering for our sin, so that we could be made right with God through Christ."

That is the most incredible offer you've ever

heard! Do you deserve it? No. Do I? No. That's why the Bible says the offer is by grace. Grace means to get what you *don't* deserve, to get *better* than you deserve. God offers it because of his love for you.

By the way, this is incredibly good news. If getting to heaven depended on me being good and meeting standards of holiness, I don't know about you, but I'd be extremely nervous. I don't think of myself as being very good, but even if I did, I'd have to wonder: *How good is good enough? Have I really met the standard?* But it's *not* about measuring up to a standard. Jesus did that for me. It's about saying yes to God's love. That's the truth, straight from the Bible.

Sandy, the Britney Spears impersonator I mentioned, showed up at my church and was shocked that no one acted "holier than thou." Everyone was very accepting and positive, and so she decided, for the first time in her life, to go back to a church a second time. And then a third. Sandy kept coming and became overwhelmed by the idea that God loved her. One time I said, "God has so much love for you," and Sandy remembers thinking, *I never knew that*. She says, "I felt it for the first time, and it opened up a whole new life for me." And Sandy's life has completely changed.

That's also what happened for Travis, who was a pimp before he said yes to God's love.

And Raul, who grew up in Las Vegas gangs.

And Brandi, who was prostituting herself to get money to support her drug habit.

And Gary, a casino pit boss who thought Christians were a bunch of hypocrites he wanted nothing to do with, until he actually showed up at our church and met some.

And Rob, who was wanted for dealing drugs.

And Warren, who was a hard-core atheist, until he realized his picture of God was of a strict disciplinarian trying to sap the joy out of people's lives, and that wasn't actually the God of the Bible.

And Jessica, who didn't know anything about God and didn't really care, until her kids started asking questions and she realized she needed answers.

And Brad, who considered himself a Buddhist until he finally took the time to really look into Christianity.

And Dallas, who was a highly paid executive for General Electric who thought people who went to church were fools, until he came to ours and realized he was wrong.

And CiCi, who was a crystal-meth addict.

They've all come to the conclusion that God is real, God's love is real, and God is really for them. And putting their faith in Jesus and letting God love them has totally changed their lives.

Your Answer

So let's get back to our two questions.

Question #1: What is your chance of getting into heaven?

Just in case I wasn't clear enough, let me make sure you now understand that there are only two possible answers to this question: 0 percent or 100 percent.

If you *have* sincerely accepted God's offer, there is a 100 percent chance that you will go to heaven. It won't matter how many bad things you've done, because the decision won't be based on your merit. It will be based completely on Jesus' merit, and he was good enough. His sheet has no sin.

If you *haven't* sincerely accepted God's offer, there is a 0 percent chance that you will go to heaven. It won't matter how many good things you've done, because the decision *will* be based on your merit, and there's no way you've been perfect. But that's what it takes to get into God's perfect heaven.

Your chance of getting into heaven: 0 percent or 100 percent. It's up to you.

Question #2: God asks, "Why should I let you into my perfect heaven?"

What will you answer?

When you considered this question earlier, you may have thought, *I'll tell God that my parents were faithful Christians*, or *I'll tell God about how often I went to church*, or *I'll tell God about how I helped out teaching children and feeding the homeless and helping old ladies across the street.* I hope it's clear now that those are the 0 percent answers. Because no matter how many good things you've done, it will never be enough to meet the standard of perfection.

The Bible says that when God asks, "Why should I let you into my perfect heaven?" sitting next to him will be his Son, Jesus. So when God asks me, I plan on pointing at Jesus and saying, "I'm with him."

It's a good answer.

God will smile and say, "Get in here. You are going to love heaven. And I'm going to love being with you."

An answer that centers on Jesus and what

he did for you on the cross is the only right answer. I just hope you give it.

You can, but only if you accept God's offer.

If someone offers you a gift, you have to decide to take it. You have to decide whether to accept the gift God is offering to you.

God is waiting for your decision.

He's waiting for *you*.

3

COMING HOME

THE BIBLE SAYS God is love. Not just that he can be loving. He *is* love.

Because he is love, God created us for relationship with him.

Because he is love, God offers us grace.

Jesus once told a story to help us understand God's love and his offer of grace.[1]

It's a story about a father who had two sons. This dad was a great and loving father, but even so, there came a point when the younger son decided he'd had enough of home. He wondered if there was something better out there, and he wanted to go looking for it. He no longer wanted to live his father's way. He was tired of being good and following the rules. He went to his father and said, "I'm leaving, and I'm never coming home. If I stayed here, when you die, you'd give me half of your inheritance, so I'd like you to just give it to me now." Basically he was saying, "Dad, I wish you were dead."

Amazingly, his father was so loving and so respected his son's free will (even to make bad choices) that he said yes and gave his son the money.

So the son set off and ended up in a faraway land, living a life that was the opposite of everything his father had ever taught him. He wasted all of his father's money on girls . . . and drinking . . . and you name it. And he sort of enjoyed it for a while, but pretty soon he was out of money. And he discovered that people weren't so interested in partying with him when he wasn't paying for the party. His life started going downhill and finally hit rock bottom when he got a job feeding pigs. It was awful. He realized that the guys who worked for his father were treated better than he was. So he decided to go home. He assumed his father would never accept him back as a son, but he hoped maybe his father would be kind enough to give him a job and let him work on the farm.

On the walk home, he practiced the speech he'd give his father when he arrived: "Father, I have sinned against heaven and against you. I am no longer worthy to be called your son, but if you'd maybe just let me work on your farm . . ."

What he didn't know was that from the moment he had left, his father had been sitting out on the front porch, staring down the road, hoping against hope, praying prayer after prayer that his son would come home. The father held this constant vigil, staring down the road, waiting for the first sign that his son was returning.

And then it happened . . . a shadow. Could it be? The father's breath was taken away. Yes, it was! And the father bolted. He went running down the street to his son.

In their culture men *never* ran—it was considered undignified. I don't know what the son was thinking when he saw his father running at him like that, but when his father got to him, the son immediately went into his speech: "Father, I have sinned . . ."

But his father grabbed him . . . and hugged him. The son wriggled free and started again, "Father, I . . ." but his speech was muffled as his father grabbed him again and wrapped him up in the biggest hug ever. Then the father shouted back to the house, "Everyone, it's happened! My son! My son is home! My son was lost, but now he's found. He was gone, but he's come home! Come bring him something nice to wear. Prepare some food, get ready to eat and dance, we're having a party! My son is home!"

That's grace. Grace means to get better than you deserve. What did that son deserve from his father? Punishment. Rejection. But he got a hug and a party. He got welcomed back into the family. And you have to wonder why. Why did the father run? Why the hug? Why the party? Why did he forgive? *Because it was his son.* If you have a child, you understand. I mean, I would do anything for one of my kids. There's nothing they could do to make me stop loving them. That's God. That's God's love.

God is a great and loving Father, and no matter where we've been or what we've done, he would do anything for us. There's nothing we can do to make him stop loving us. And so God offers us far better than we deserve, and *that's grace.* We can't earn anything from God. We just accept it.

We come home.

By the way, this is what makes Christianity different from the way any human being would approach God and different from every other world religion. It's this idea of grace.

Humans believe we need to be deserving. We would never come up with grace.

If you study the other religions of the world, you'll see that *none* of them have this idea of grace. The core idea of every other world religion is that we have to *earn* favor from God—through our good works, by not sinning too much. Only Christianity says we can't earn it, but God loves us so much that he will forgive us and give us his good favor as a gift.

This is where the story Jesus told got really interesting. It seemed like the story was over, with the joyful return of the younger son. But right as the father was announcing the party, the older son entered the story. He said, "What's going on here?" Dad said, "Your brother, my son—he's home. We're having a party!" The older son said, "But *I've* worked for you. *I've* labored for you. *I've* never disobeyed. *I've* earned the party."

That's the natural way humans approach God. That's every other world religion. For them it's all about laboring for God, trying not to disobey, and earning God's favor. Christianity is the opposite: it's about grace; it says God loves you simply because you're his child. He loves you no matter what you've done.

And that's what the father said to this older son. He said, "Earned it? What do you mean? You're my son. You can't earn my love. I love you . . . just because you're my son. And your brother here—he couldn't lose my love, because he's my son." That's Christianity. That's God.

God is love. God's love is perfect. There's nothing you could ever do to make him love you any more than he does right now. And there's nothing you could ever do to make him love you any less. You're not perfect, but his love for you is.

So no matter why you left, no matter where

you went, no matter what you've done, no matter what you've become, God is inviting you to come home. He's waiting to forgive you. He's offering his love to you. He wants a relationship with you. And you have a choice to make.

Unless you have already come to the realization that your life without God is not what you want it to be,

> unless you've already taken the journey home,
>
> unless you've already expressed your repentance to God,
>
> unless you've already felt his embrace and received his forgiveness,
>
> God is waiting for you.
>
> The most important decision of your life awaits.

I can't think of any reason why you wouldn't say yes. All the things you've really been looking for, you'll find if you look to God.

Say yes. Tell him.

If you've said yes in the past, understand that God offers his invitation to you to come home every single day. And he wants us to accept it again every single day.

I find that I have a lot of days when I'm too busy or too distracted to come home to God.

I also have days when I feel too dirty or too guilty to come home to God.

But there is nothing in any far-off land better than what my Father is offering me at home.

And there's nothing I've done to put myself out of the reach of his grace.

So I listen, and I hear God calling out to me: Come home.

Listen, because God is calling to you. He's been inviting you every day of your life; he is inviting you today; his call will go out to you every day of your future.

Come home.

NOW WHAT?

MAYBE THIS LITTLE BOOK has led you to want to let God love you, to put your faith in Jesus, to come home. Or perhaps you're not quite there yet, but you do feel like you're headed in that direction. What do you do now? Here are a few suggestions:

1. Read the Bible. As you read God's book, you'll get to know God. Not only will

you gain head knowledge, but your heart will be drawn to him. So what do you read in the Bible? I would suggest reading the New Testament (the part after Jesus comes) before you read the Old Testament (the part before Jesus comes). The New Testament will feel more relevant to your life and will help you understand the Old Testament when you start reading it.

My church provides a Bible-reading plan that has you read one chapter of the New Testament each weekday, taking you through the entire New Testament in a year, and one chapter of the Old Testament every weekend day, taking you through the entire Old Testament over several years. We also provide a daily blog post (which you can have e-mailed to you) providing a little background on the chapter you're reading as well as some questions to help you apply it to your

life. You can learn more and subscribe
to receive the daily posts via e-mail at
http://www.vervecatalysts.org/p/bible
-reading-plan.html.

2. Pray. Don't be intimidated by the idea
of prayer; it's just talking to God. Prayer
is sharing your heart with him and
inviting him to share his heart with
you. Ideally, you want to talk with God
throughout your day, all day. The best
way to move toward that is to start each
day with a focused time of prayer. My
church provides some ideas on how
you might approach this prayer time at
http://www.vervecatalysts.org/p/prayer
-plan.html.

3. Find a church to join. God doesn't want
us to do life alone. The reality is that we
need other people walking with us on
our spiritual journey, because consistently
moving in the right direction is challeng-
ing. I encourage you to look for a church

that teaches that Jesus is the only way
to heaven (because he is) and that the
Bible is the Word of God (because it is),
that will allow you to get connected with
other believers (because you need that),
and that you'd feel comfortable inviting
your non-believing friends to (because
they need that).

If I can help you on your journey, I'd love to.
E-mail me at vince@vivalaverve.org.

NOTES

DEAD PEOPLE

1. I believe I first heard this idea expressed this way by pastor and writer Steven Furtick.
2. See John 13:35.
3. Michael J. Brown, "First God Loves Us," in *God's Man: A Daily Devotional Guide to Christlike Character*, 2nd ed., ed. Don M. Aycock (Grand Rapids, MI: Kregel, 2000), 15.

SWITCHING SHEETS

1. I also used this story in *I Became a Christian and All I Got Was This Lousy T-Shirt*, published by Baker Books, a division of Baker Publishing Group, 2008. Used here by permission.
2. See Deuteronomy 4:24; Isaiah 10:17-18; Hebrews 12:29.
3. See Matthew 5:21-30.
4. David Platt, *Follow Me* (Carol Stream, IL: Tyndale, 2013), 31-32.

COMING HOME

1. You can read this story in Luke 15:11-32.

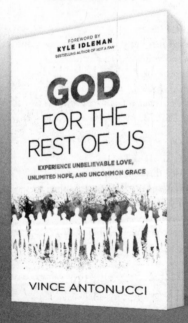

The Pharisees called Jesus,

"a friend of sinners."

He took it as a compliment. What would they
call us today? Join the conversation.

TheRestOfUsResources.com

EXPERIENCE. TRUTH.

CITYONAHILLSTUDIO.COM

>>> LEARN MORE

WANT TO LEARN MORE ABOUT VINCE'S CHURCH FOR PEOPLE WHO DON'T LIKE CHURCH AND HOW YOU CAN PARTNER WITH THEM?

VIVALAVERVE.ORG

WANT TO LEARN MORE ABOUT THE MOVEMENT VINCE'S CHURCH IS LAUNCHING TO PLANT CHURCHES IN SINFUL PLACES FOR CYNICAL PEOPLE?

SPLAGNA.COM